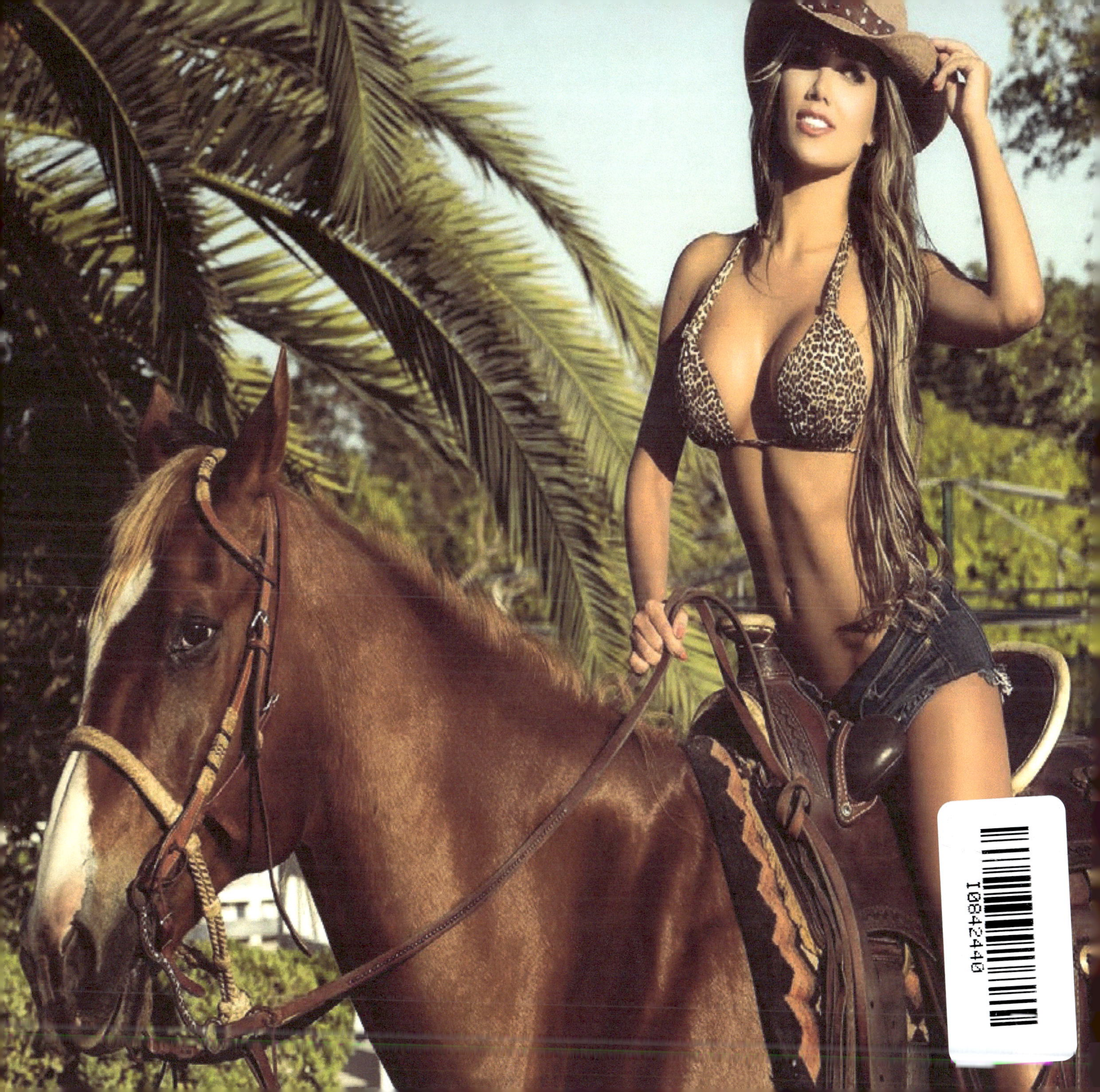
I0842440

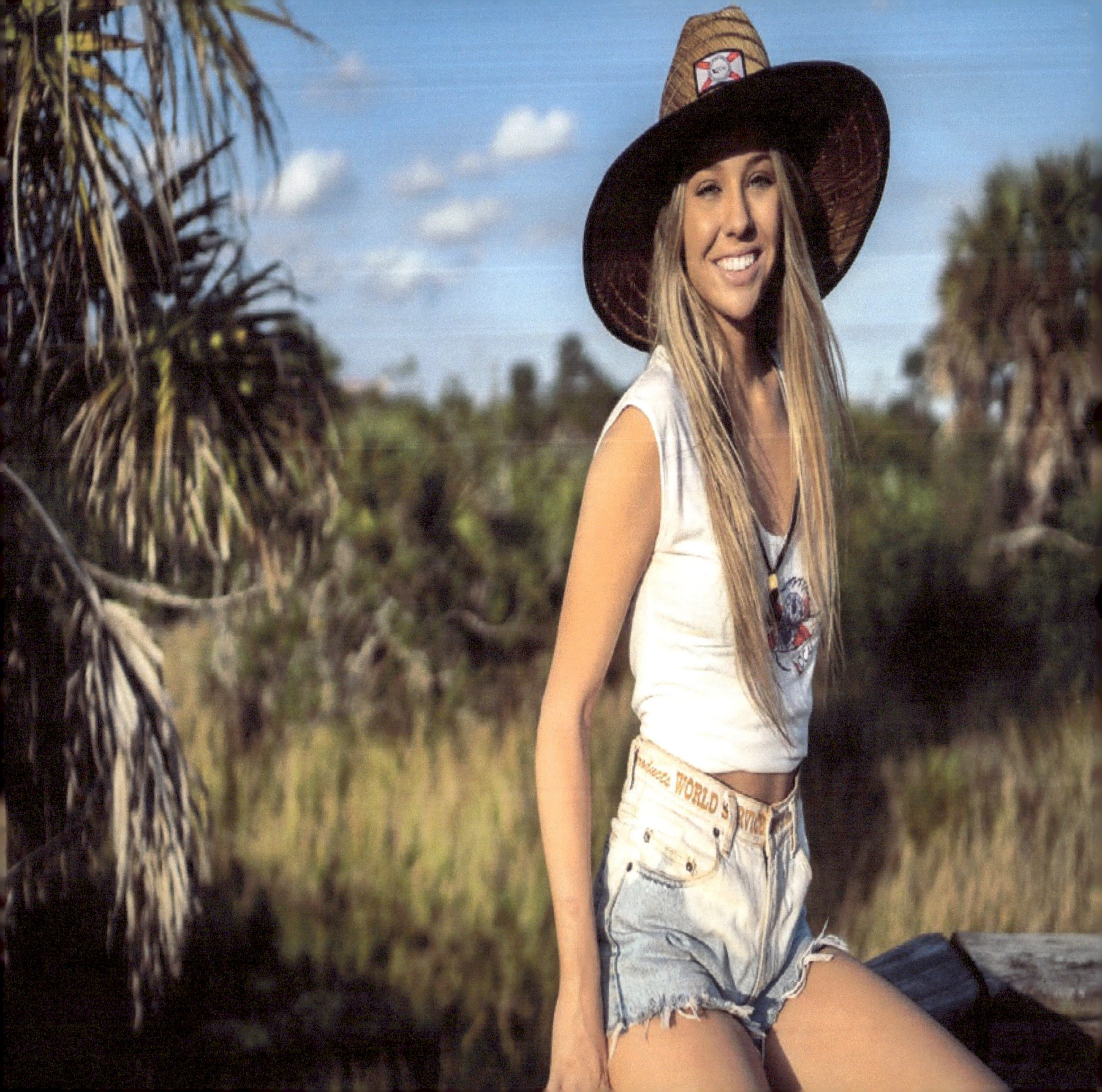

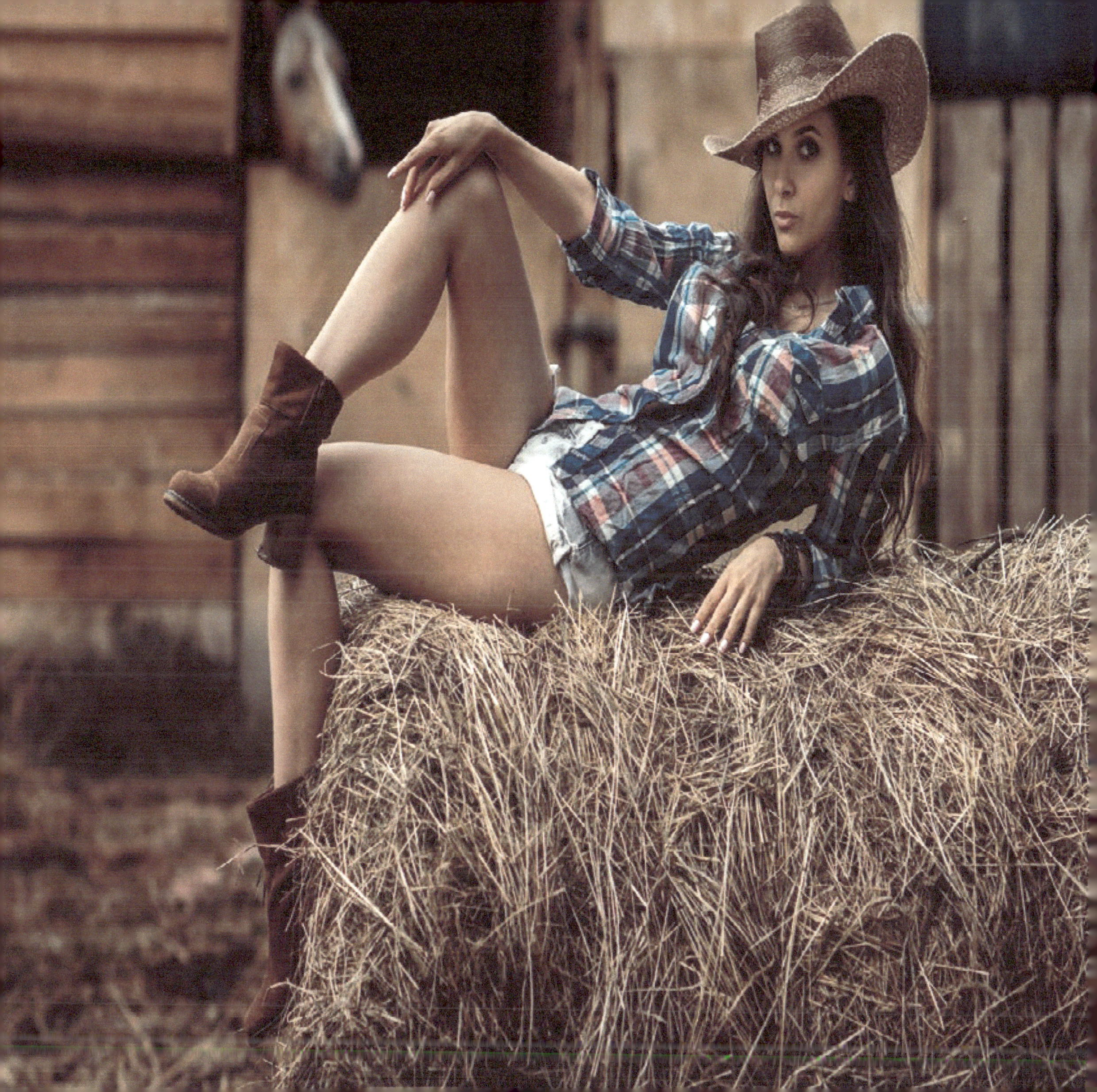

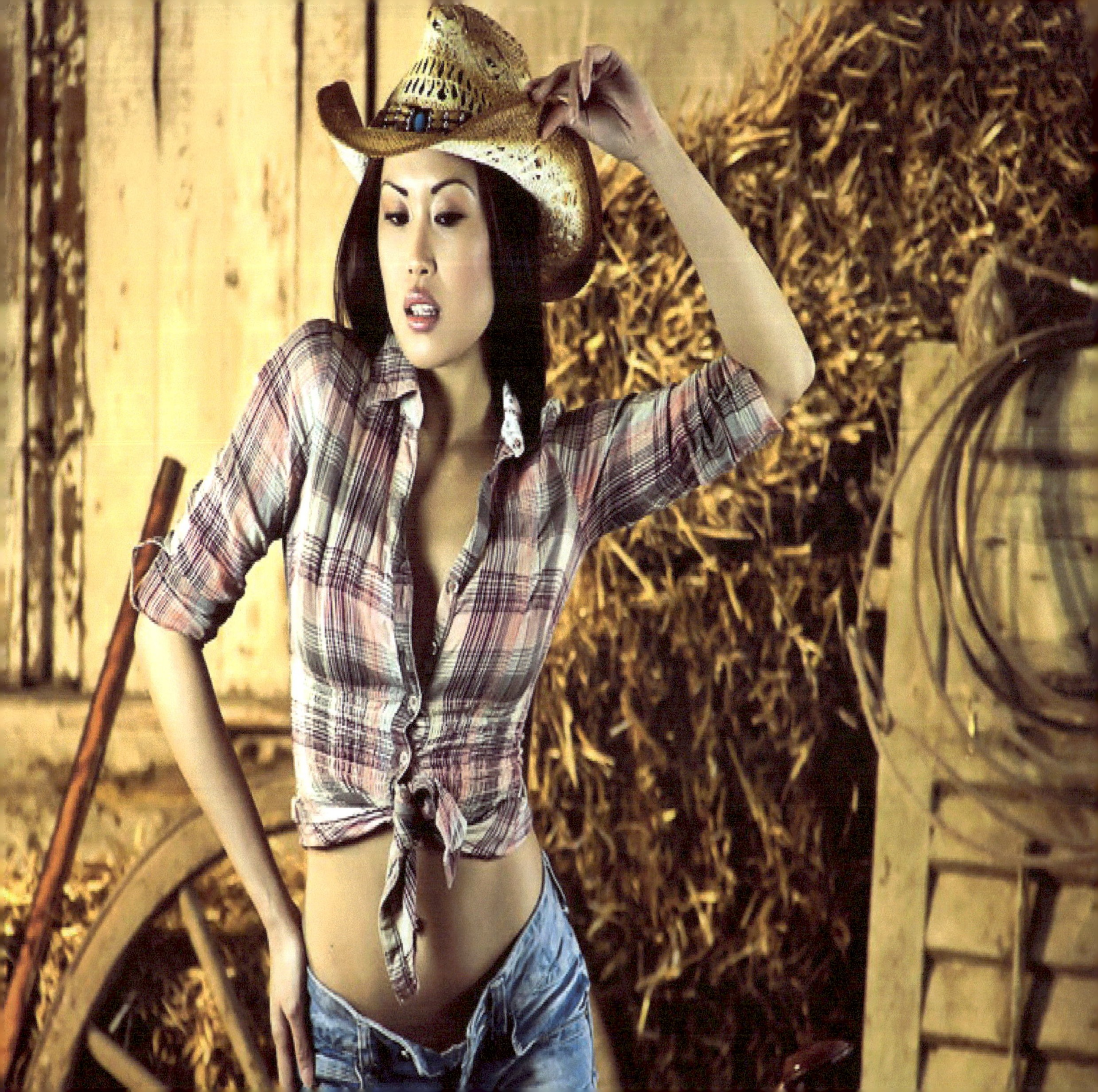

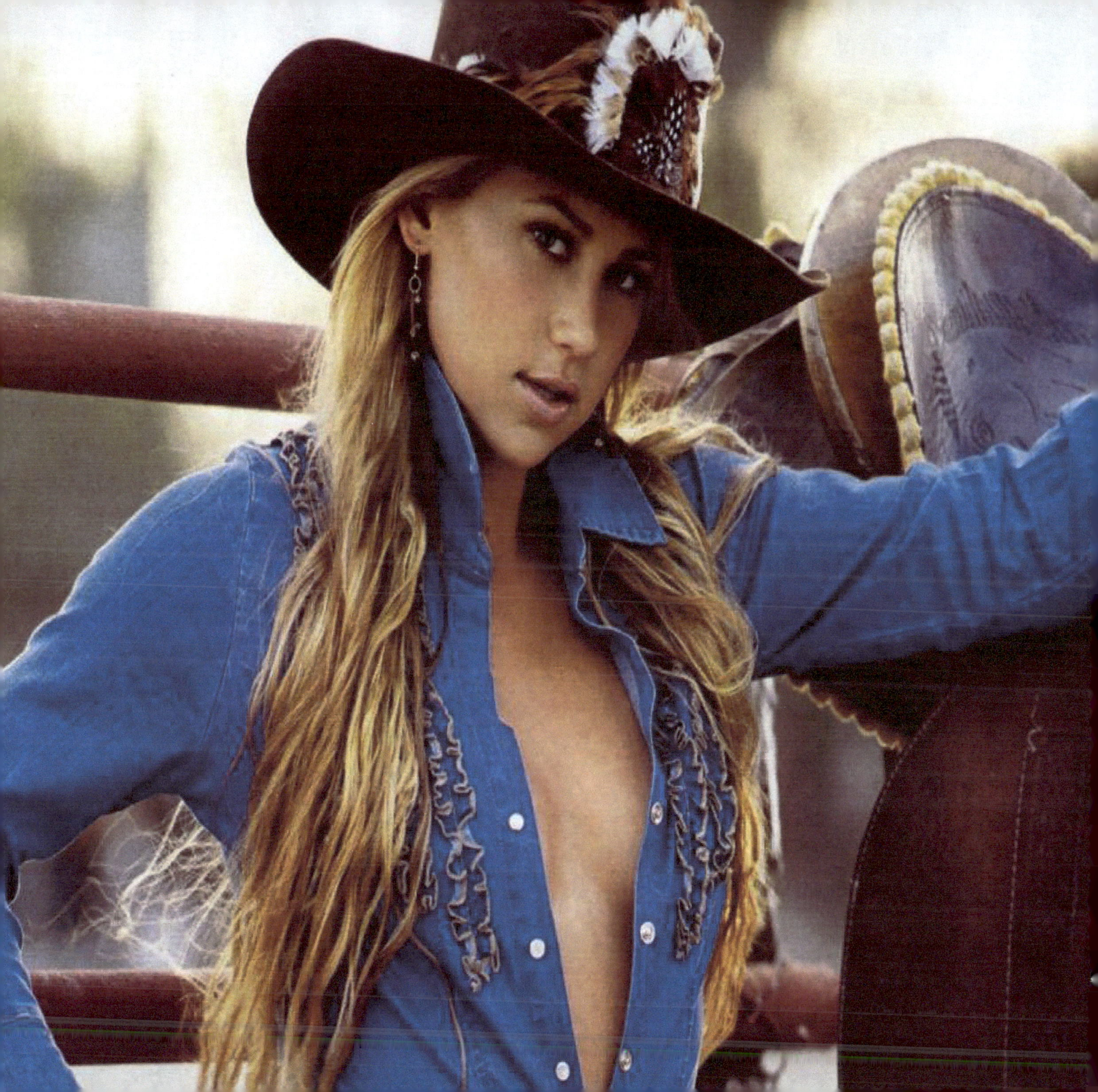

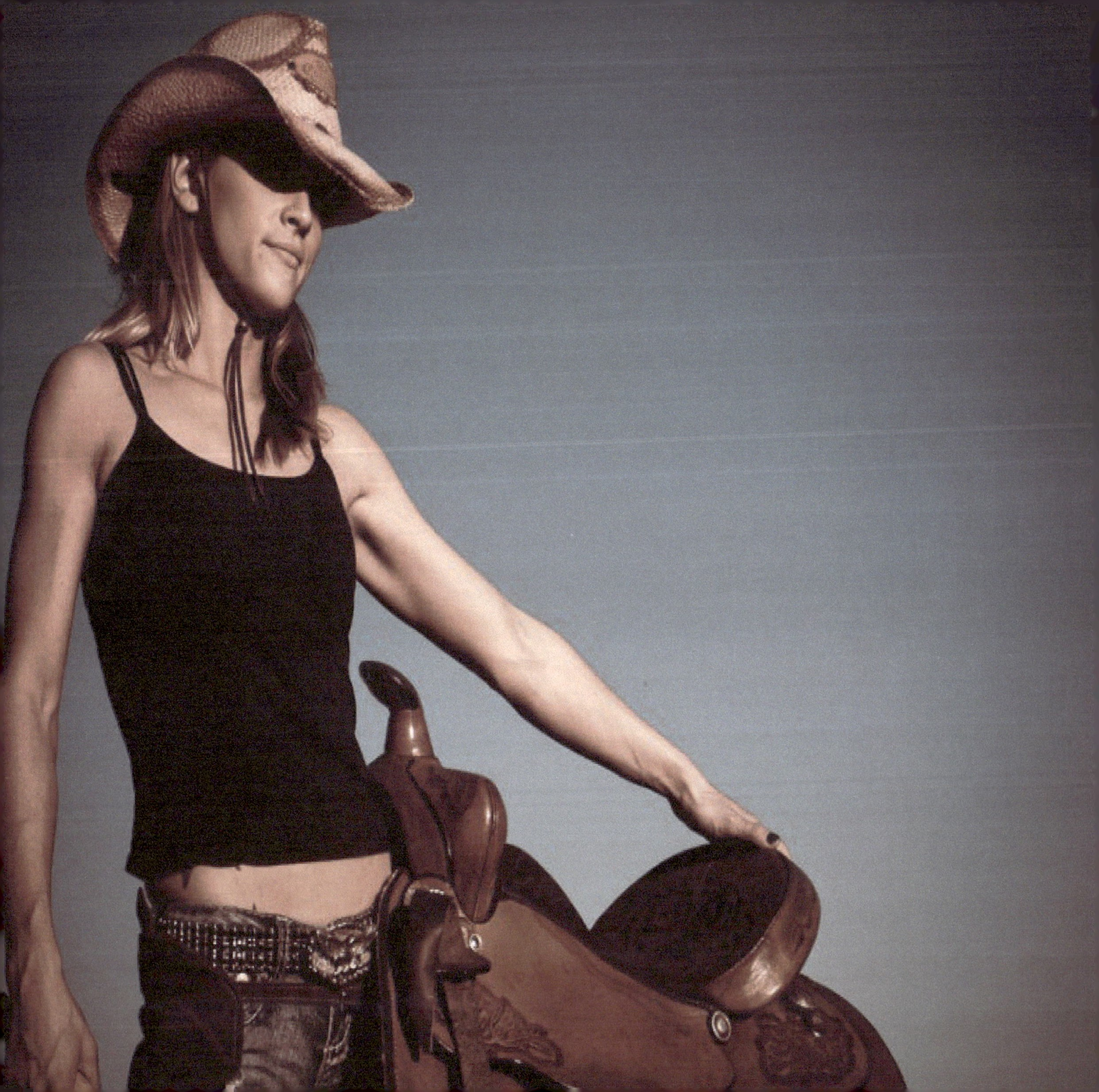

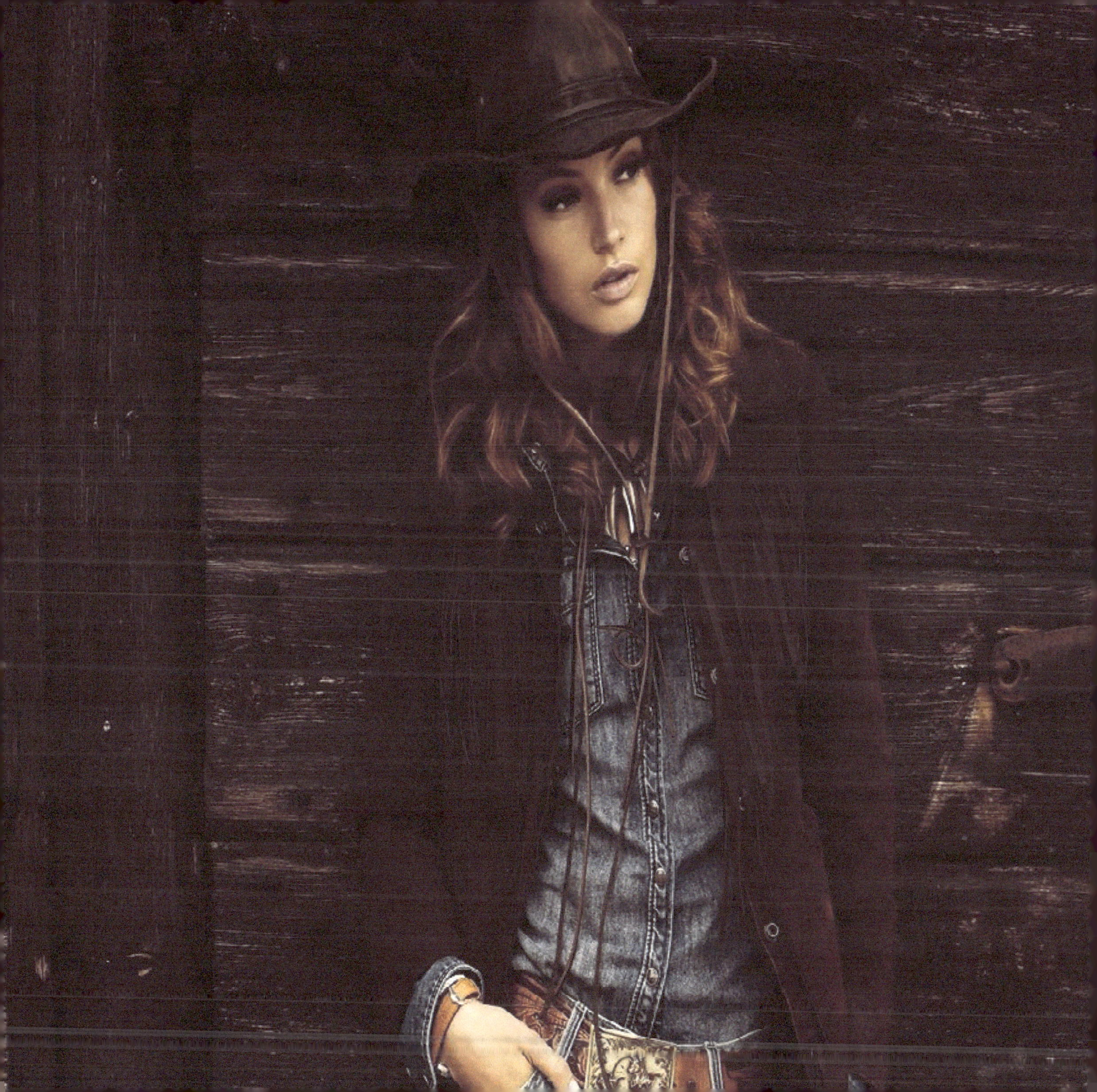

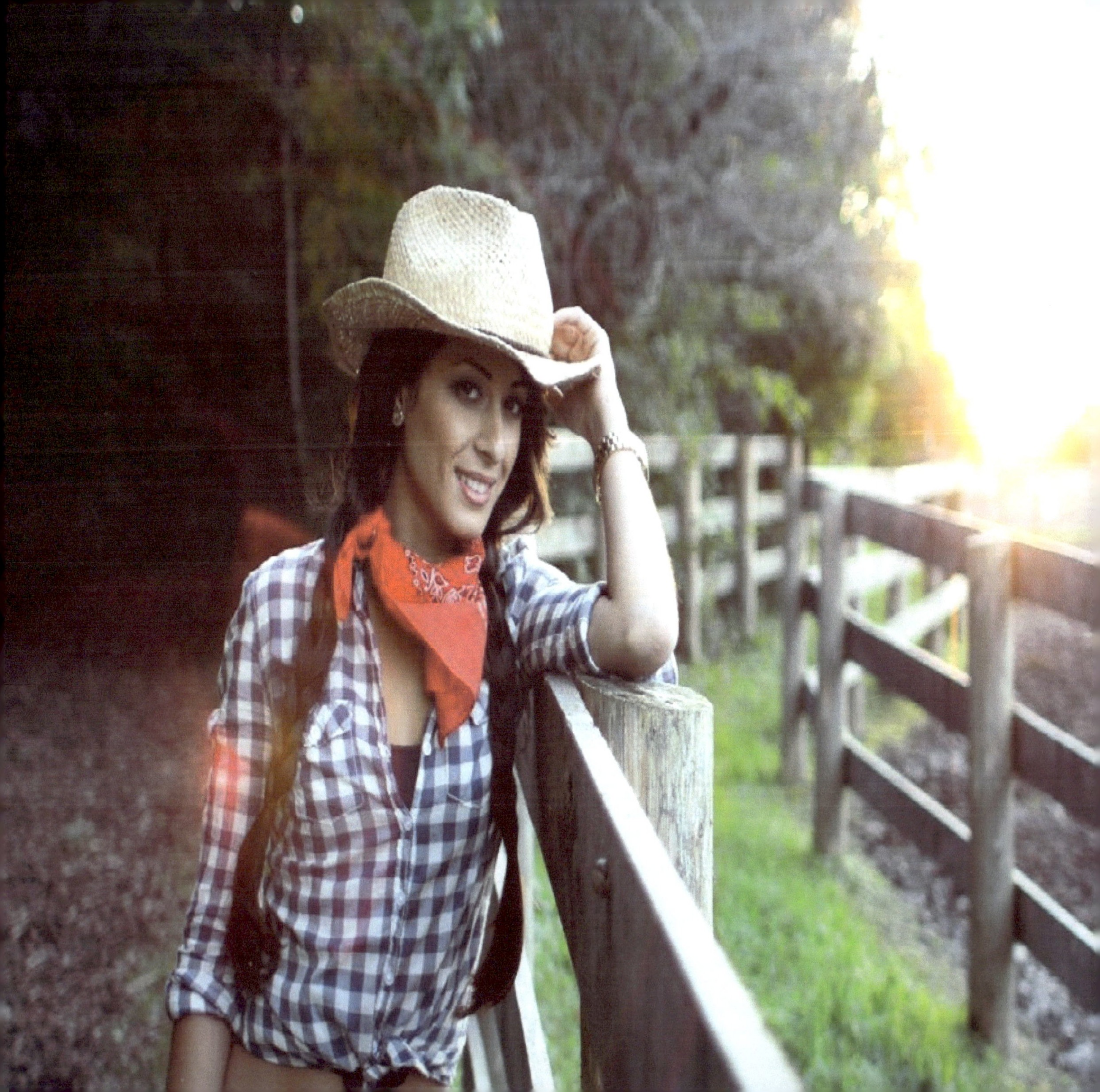

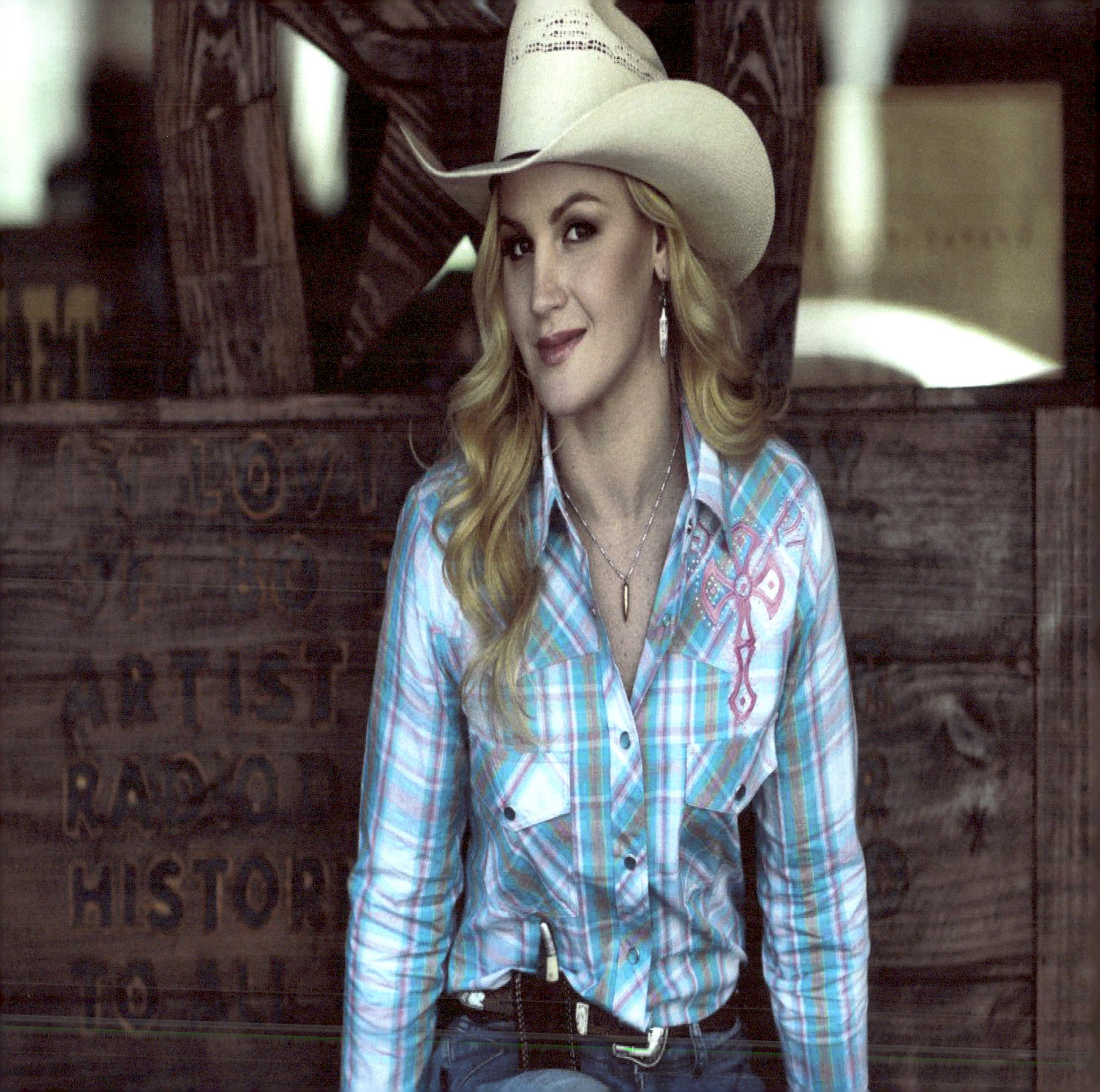
LOV
ARTIST
RADIO
HISTORY
TO ALL

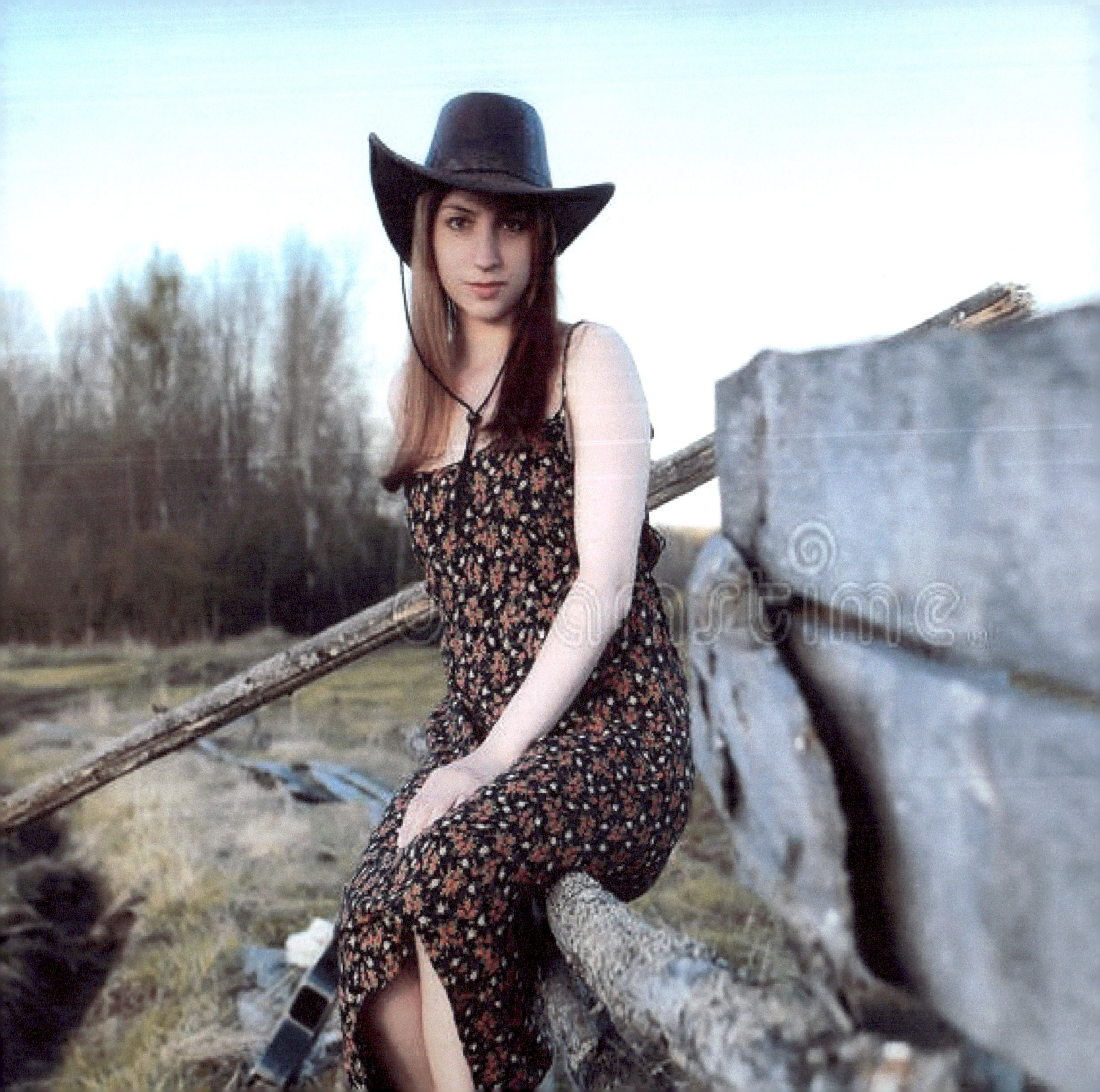

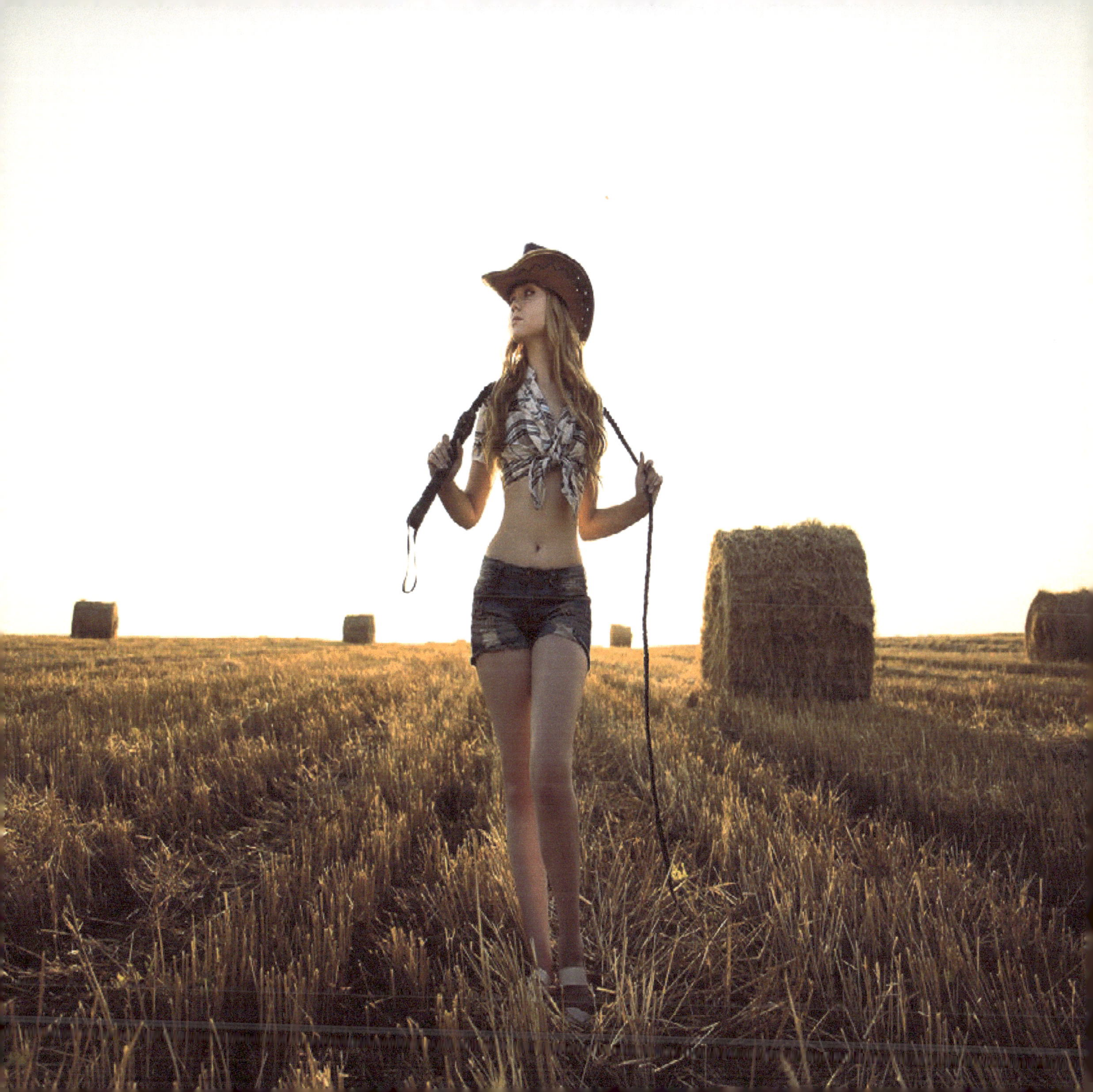

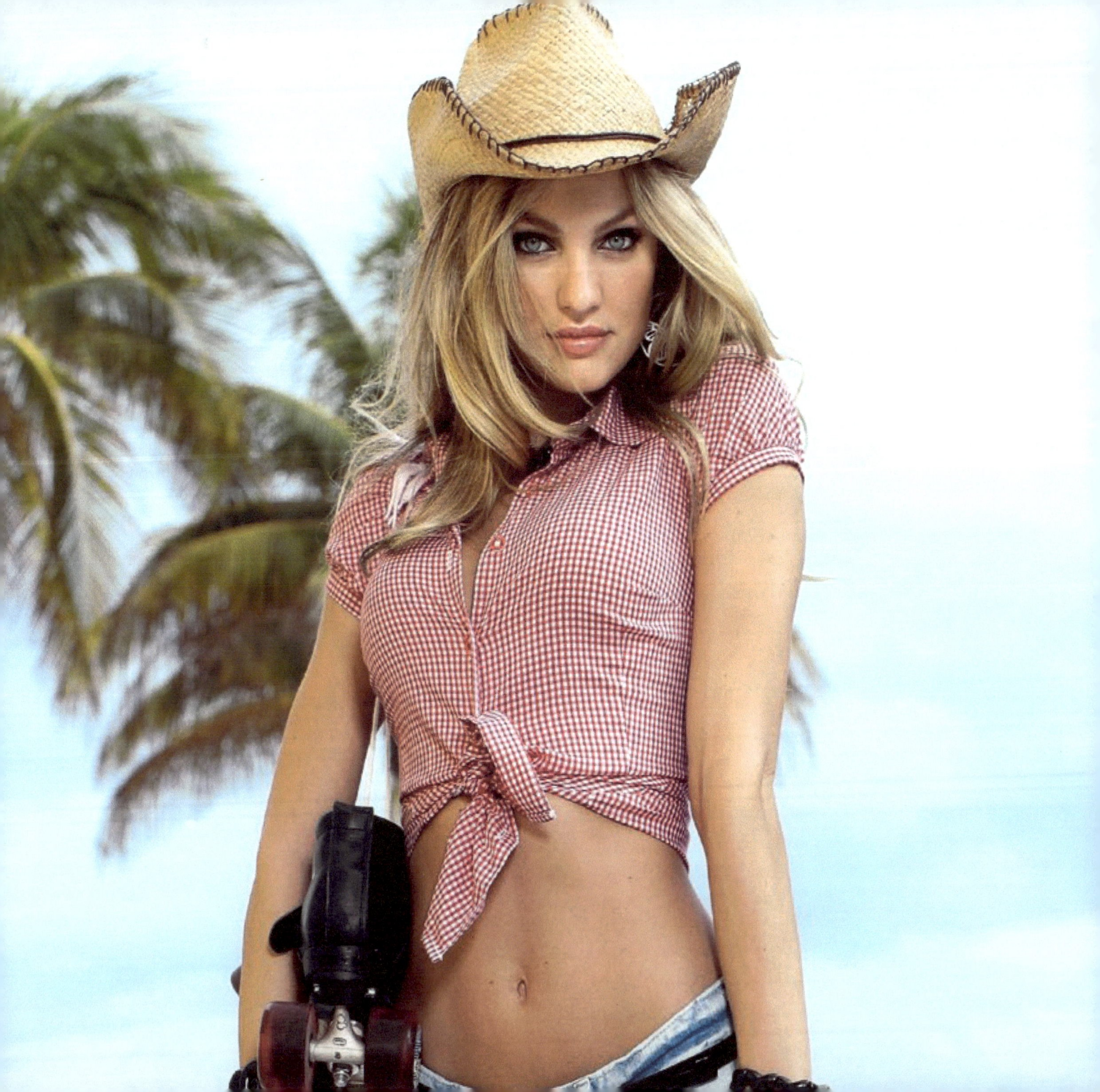

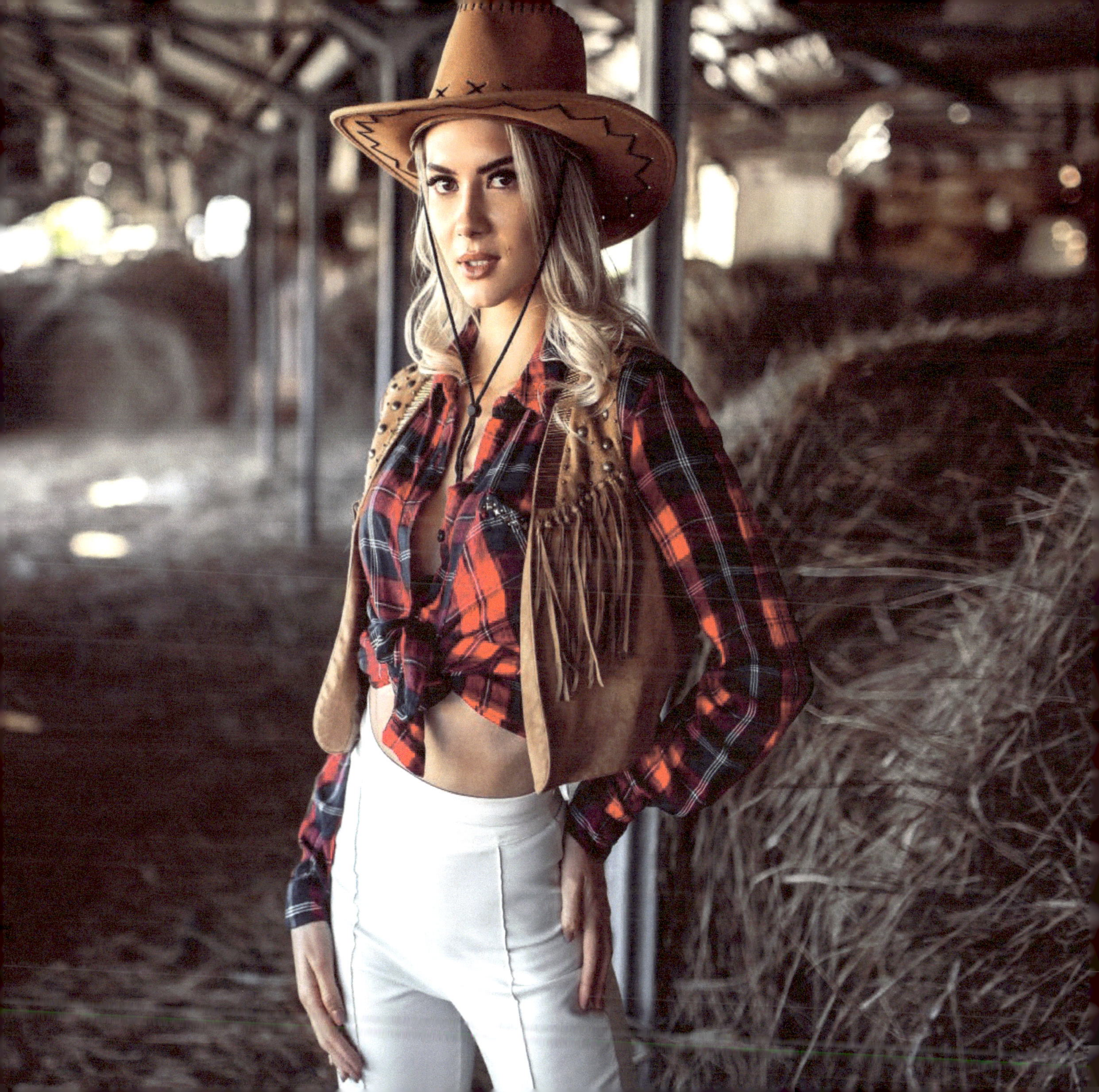

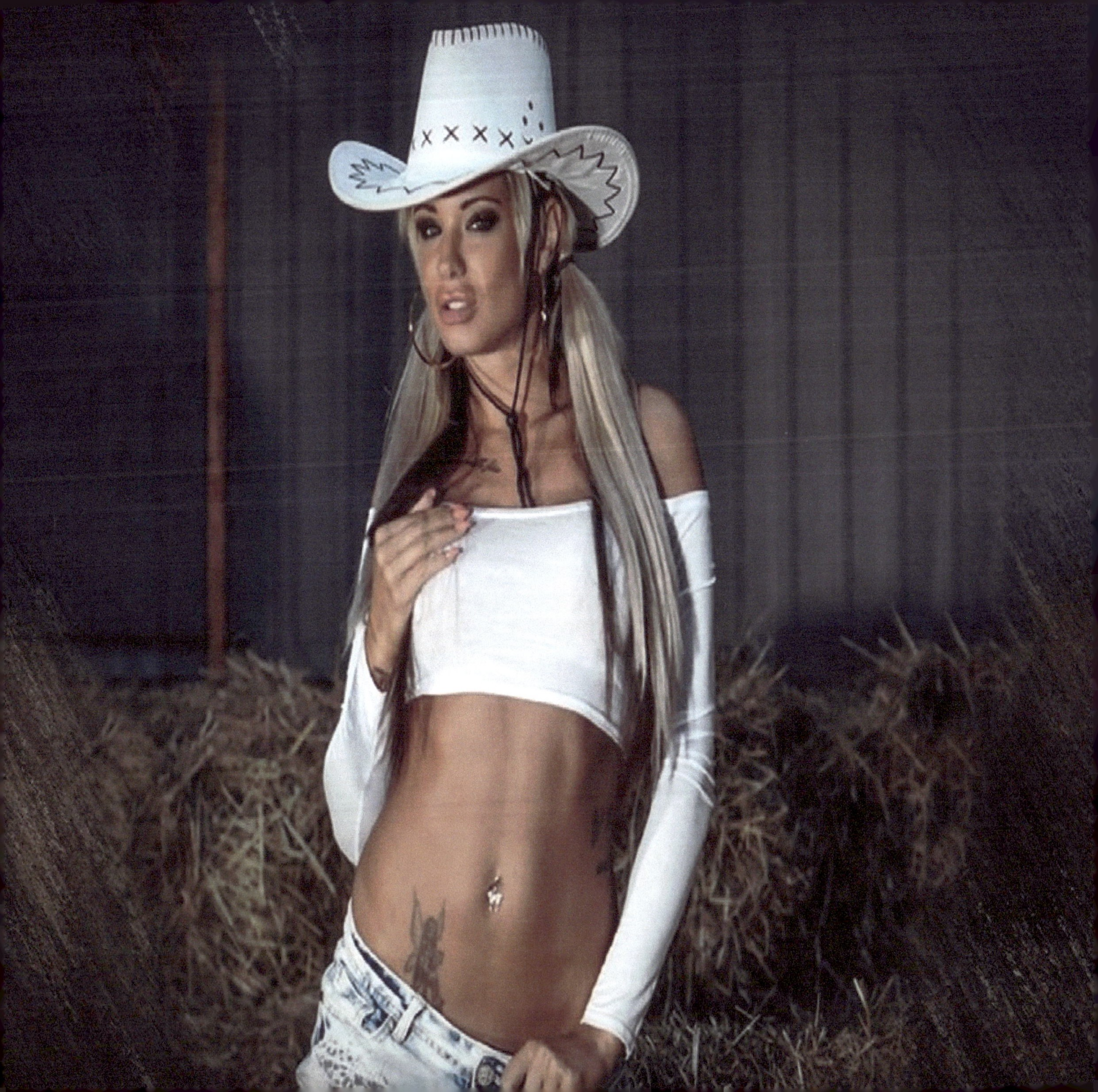

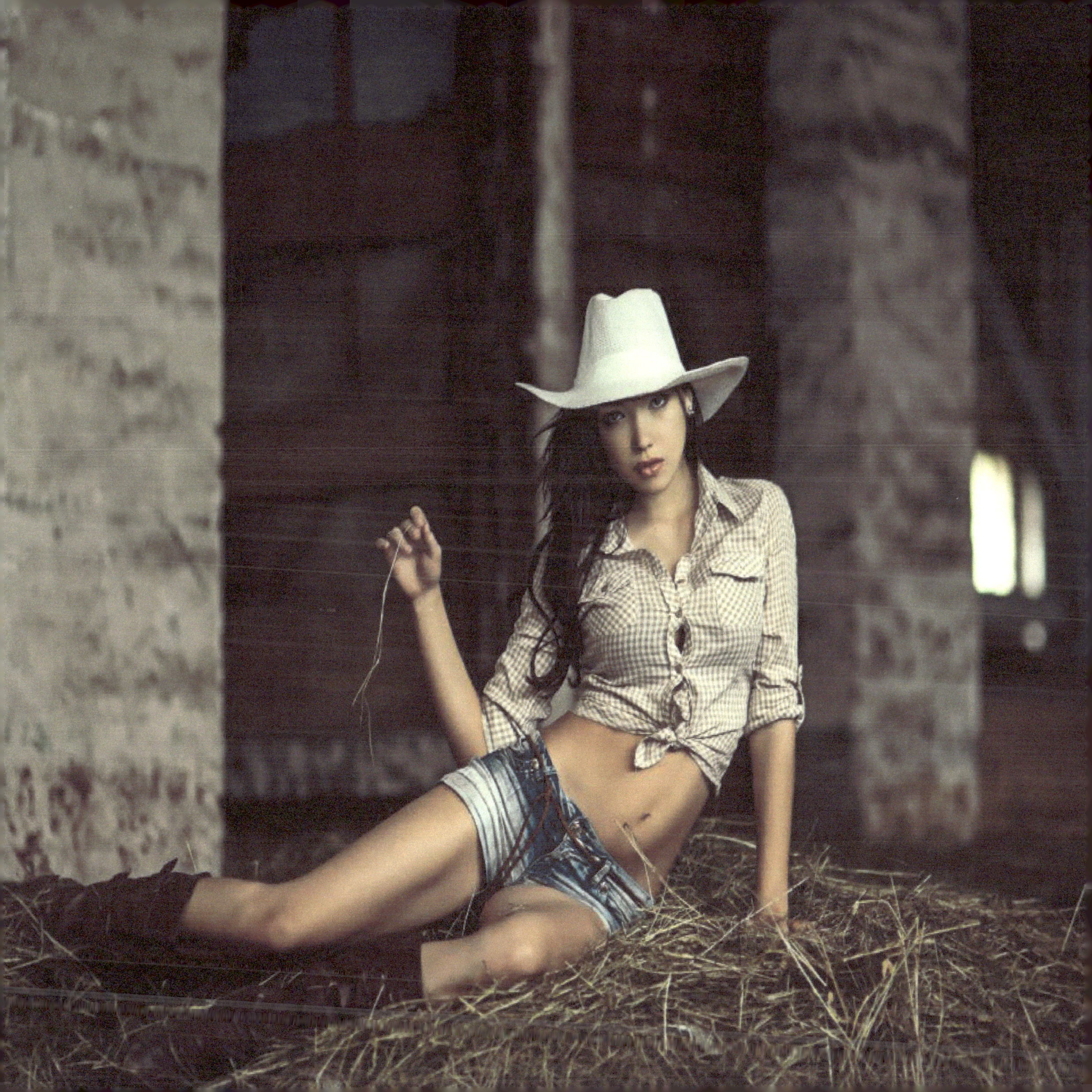

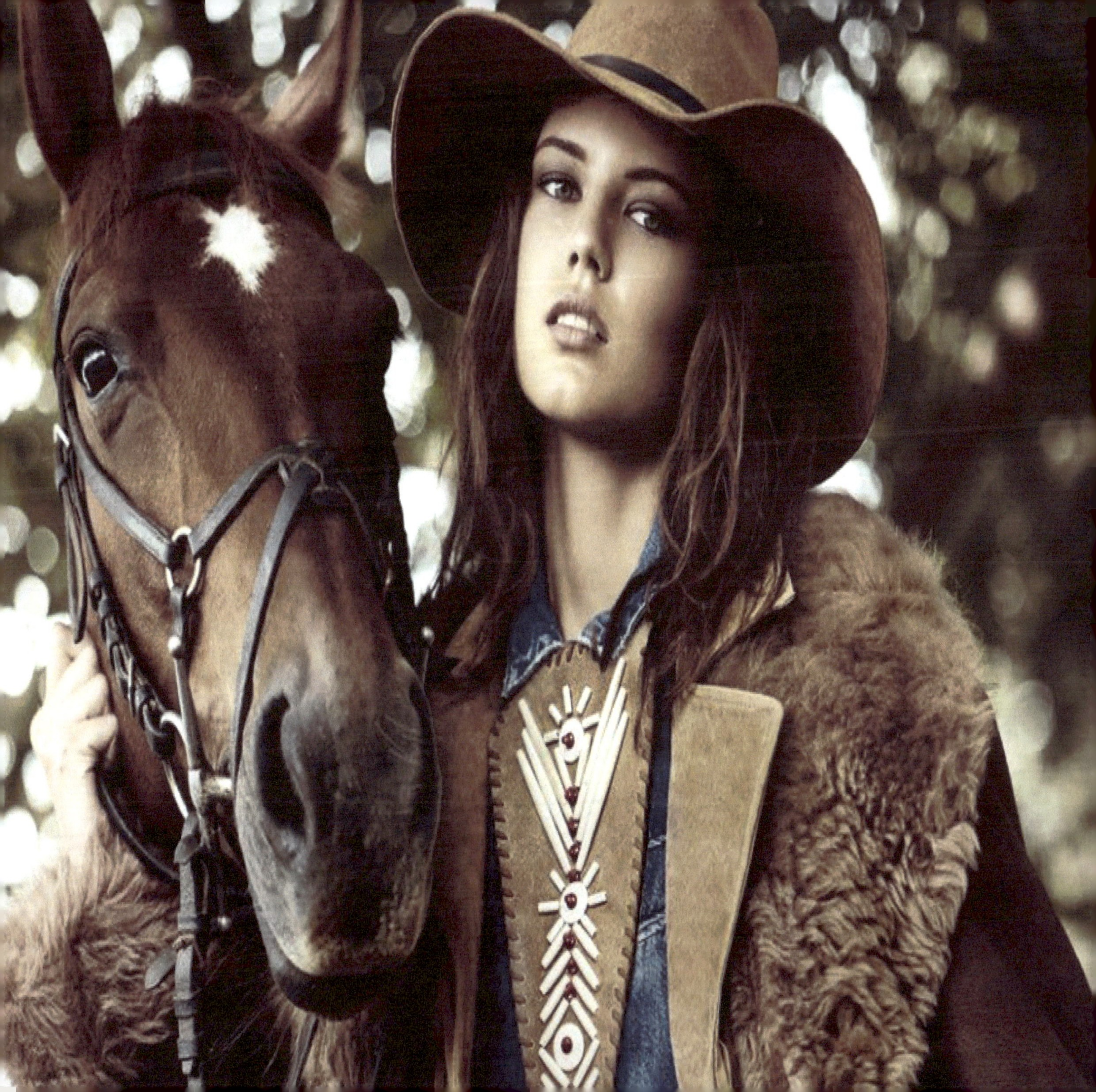

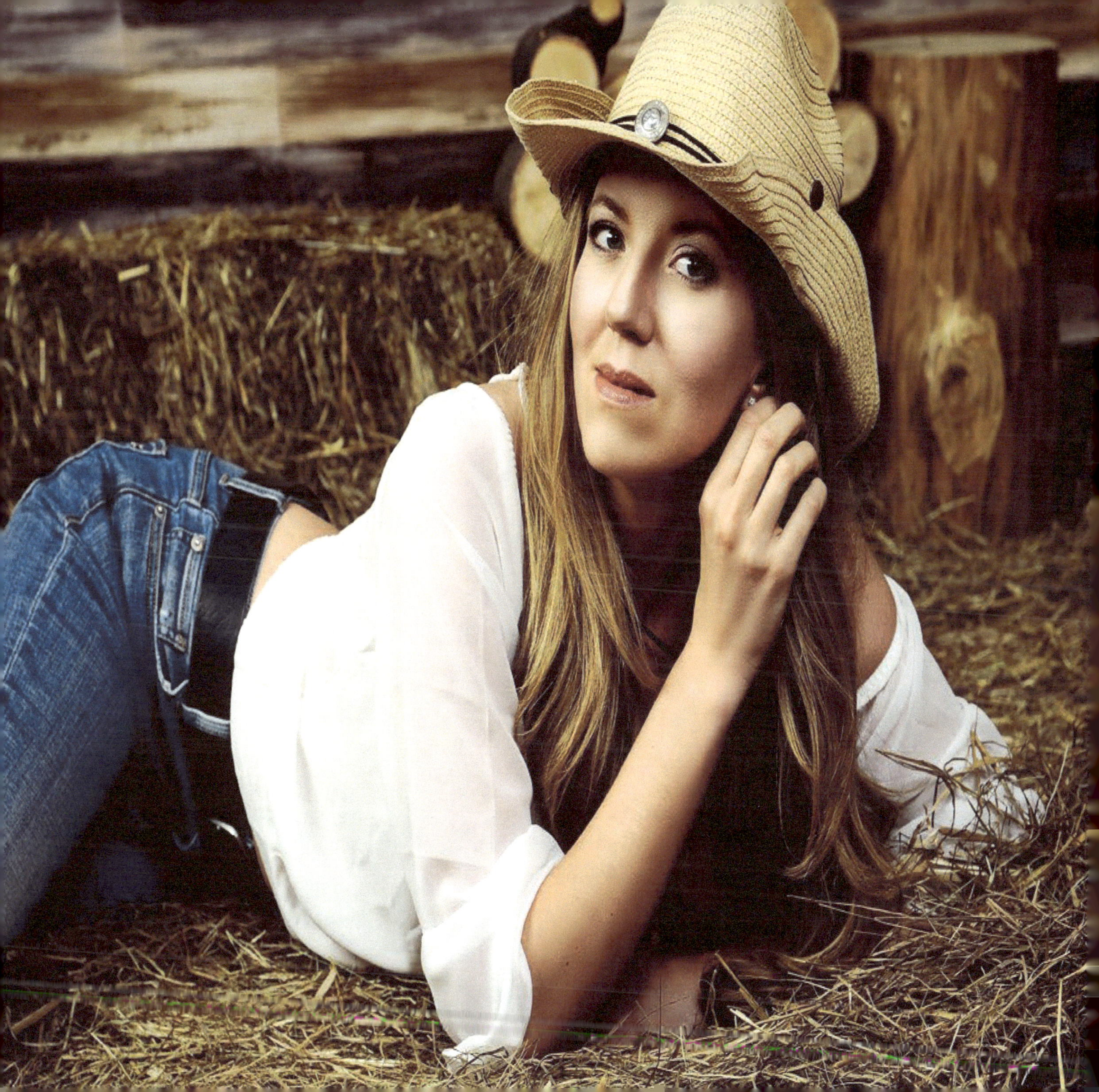

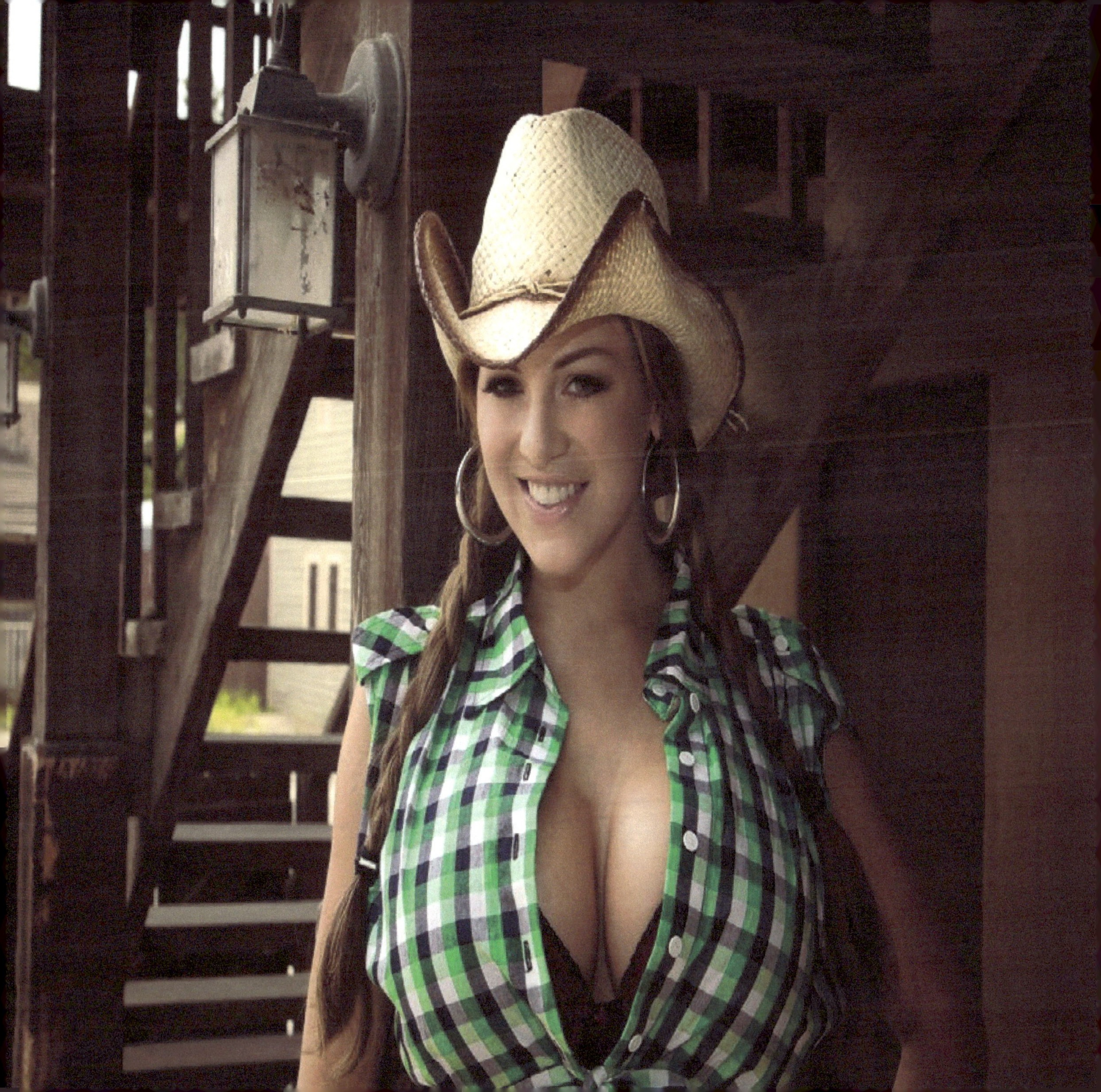

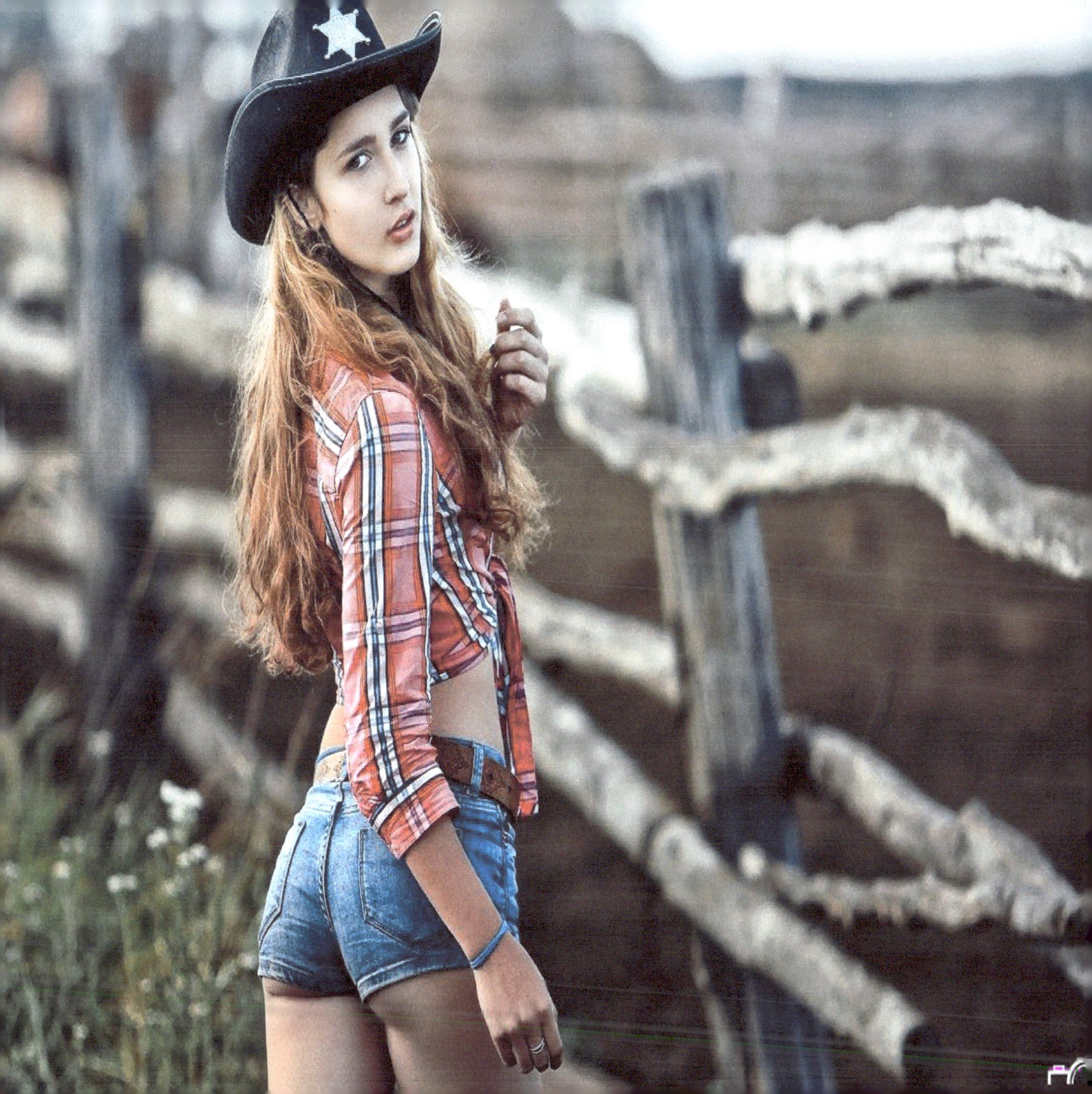

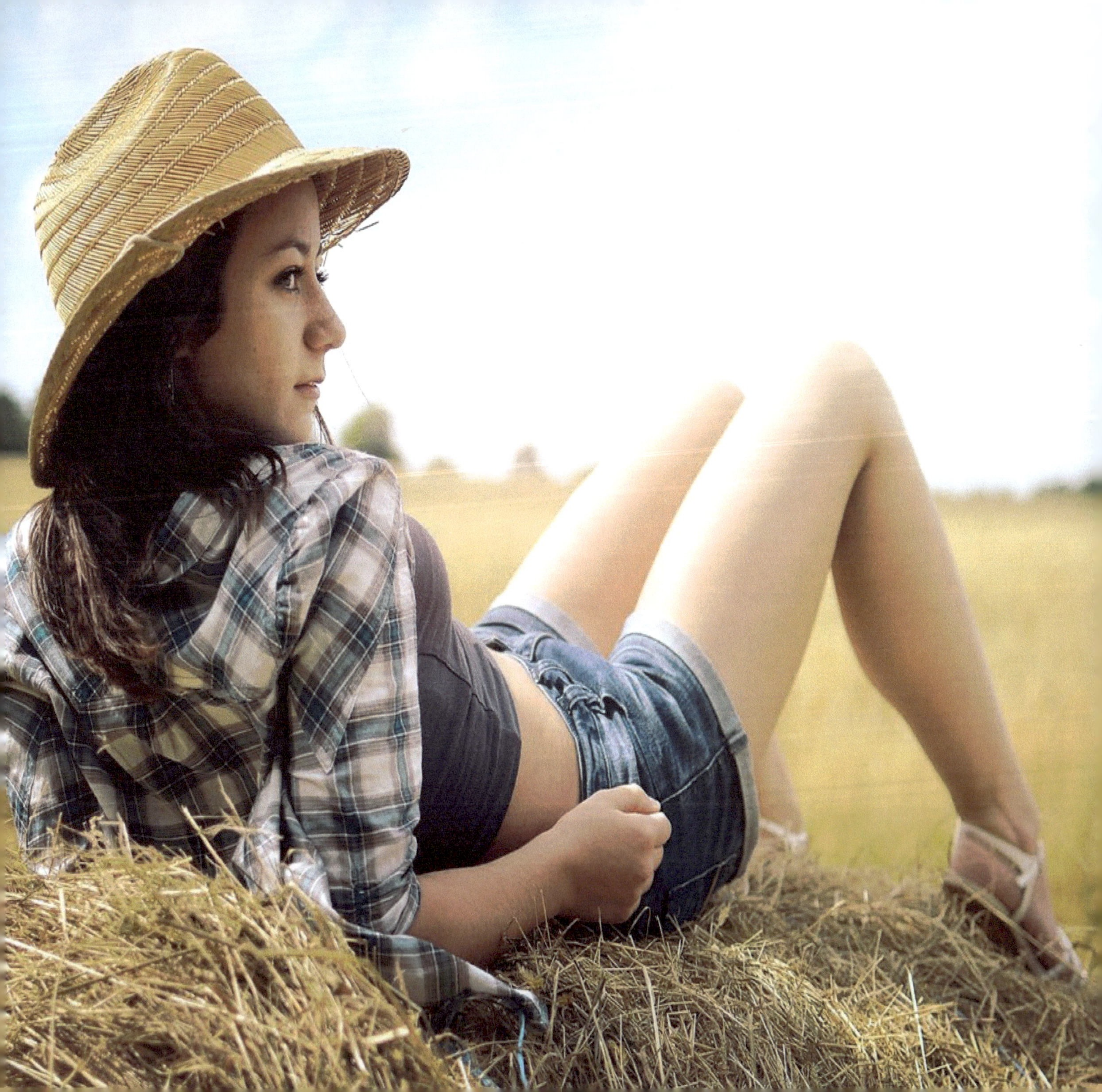

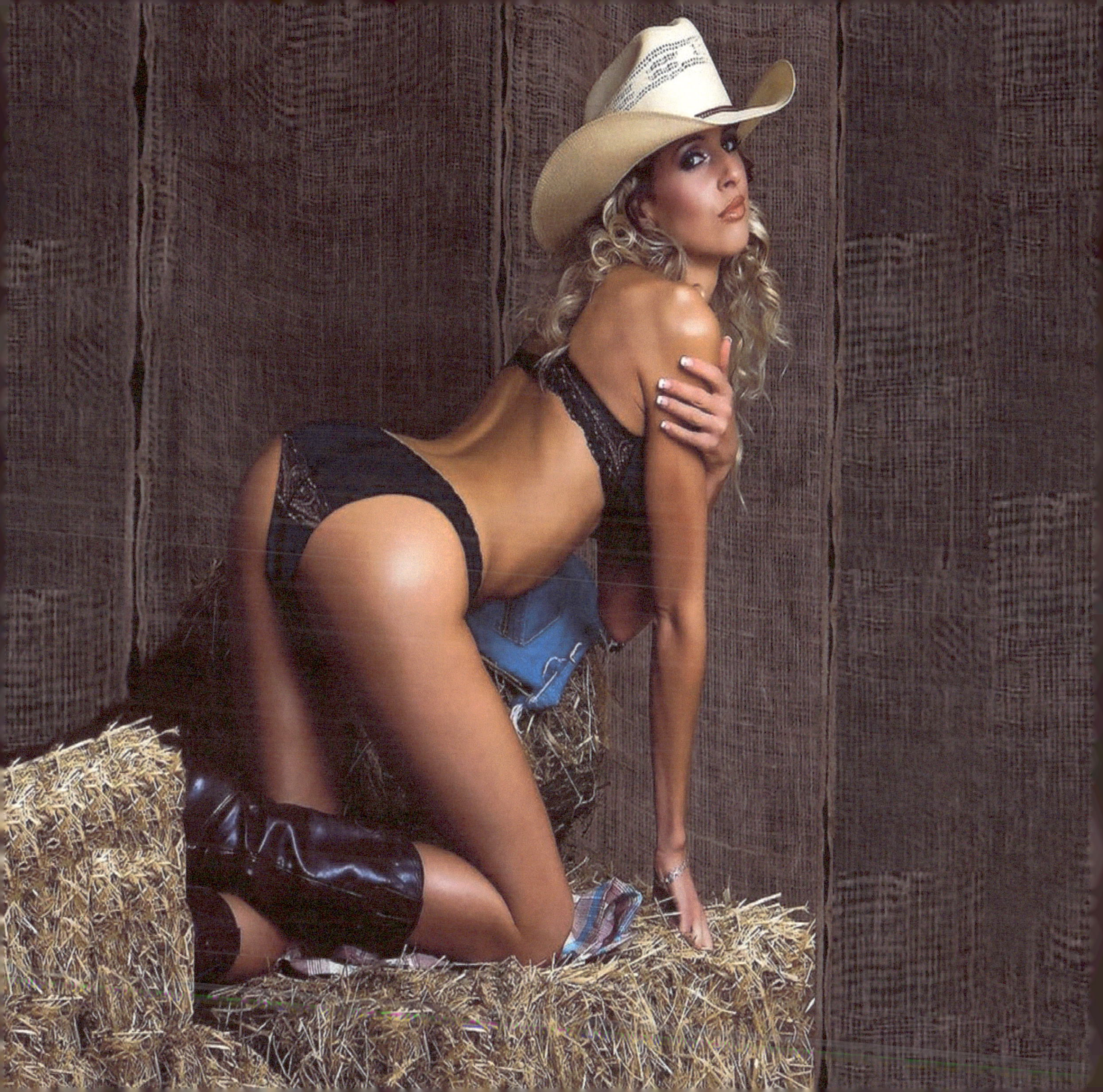

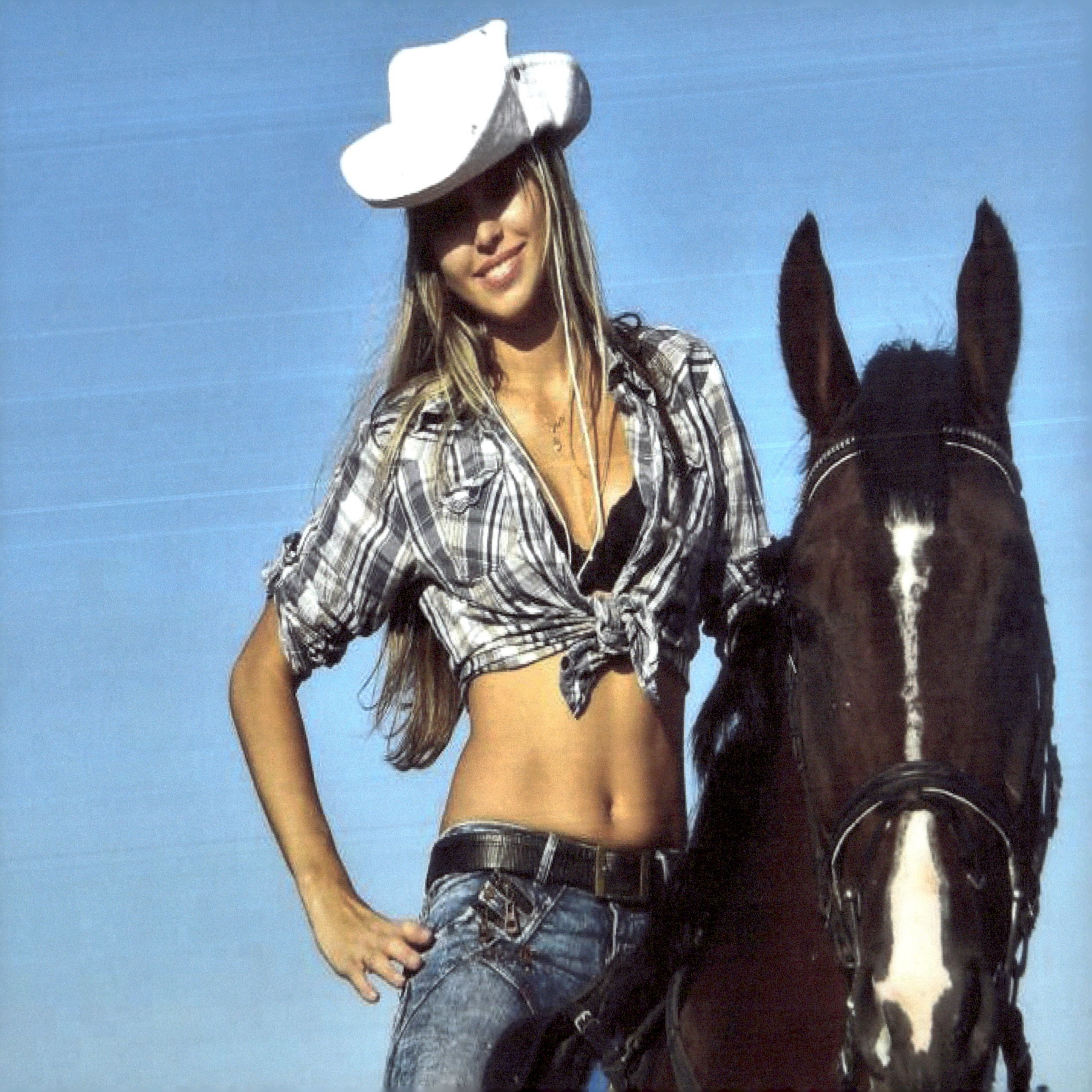

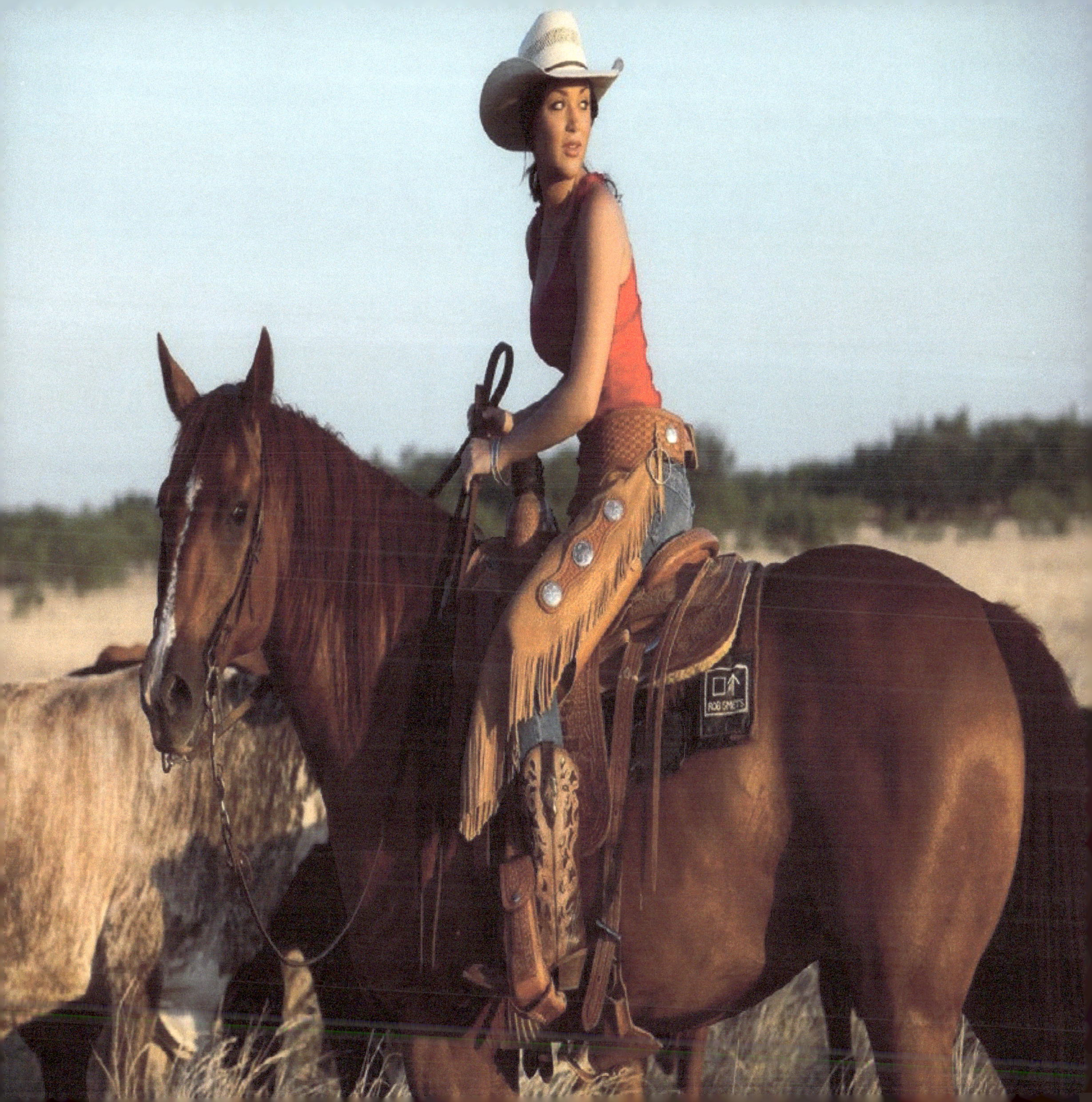
ROB SMETS

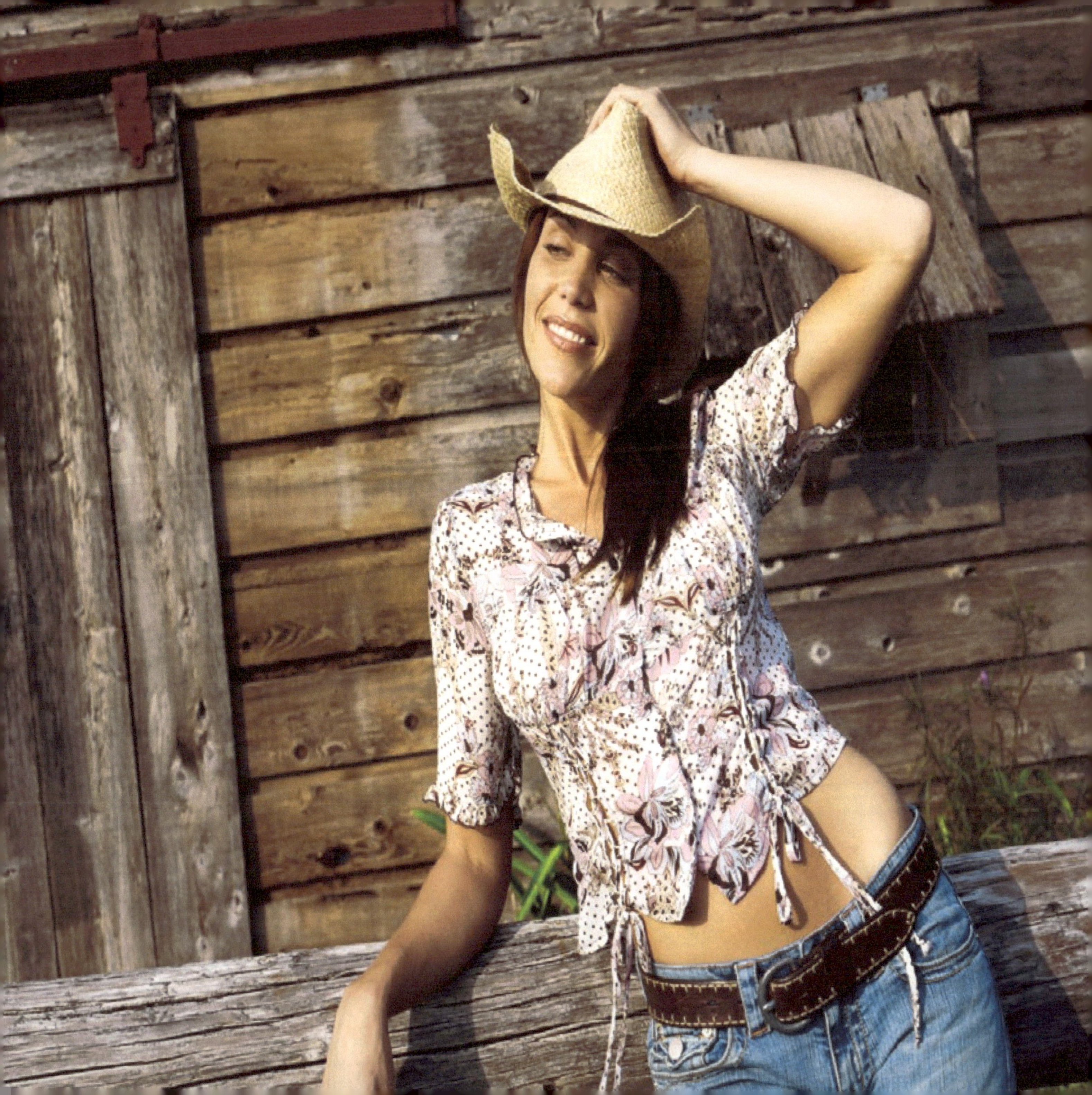

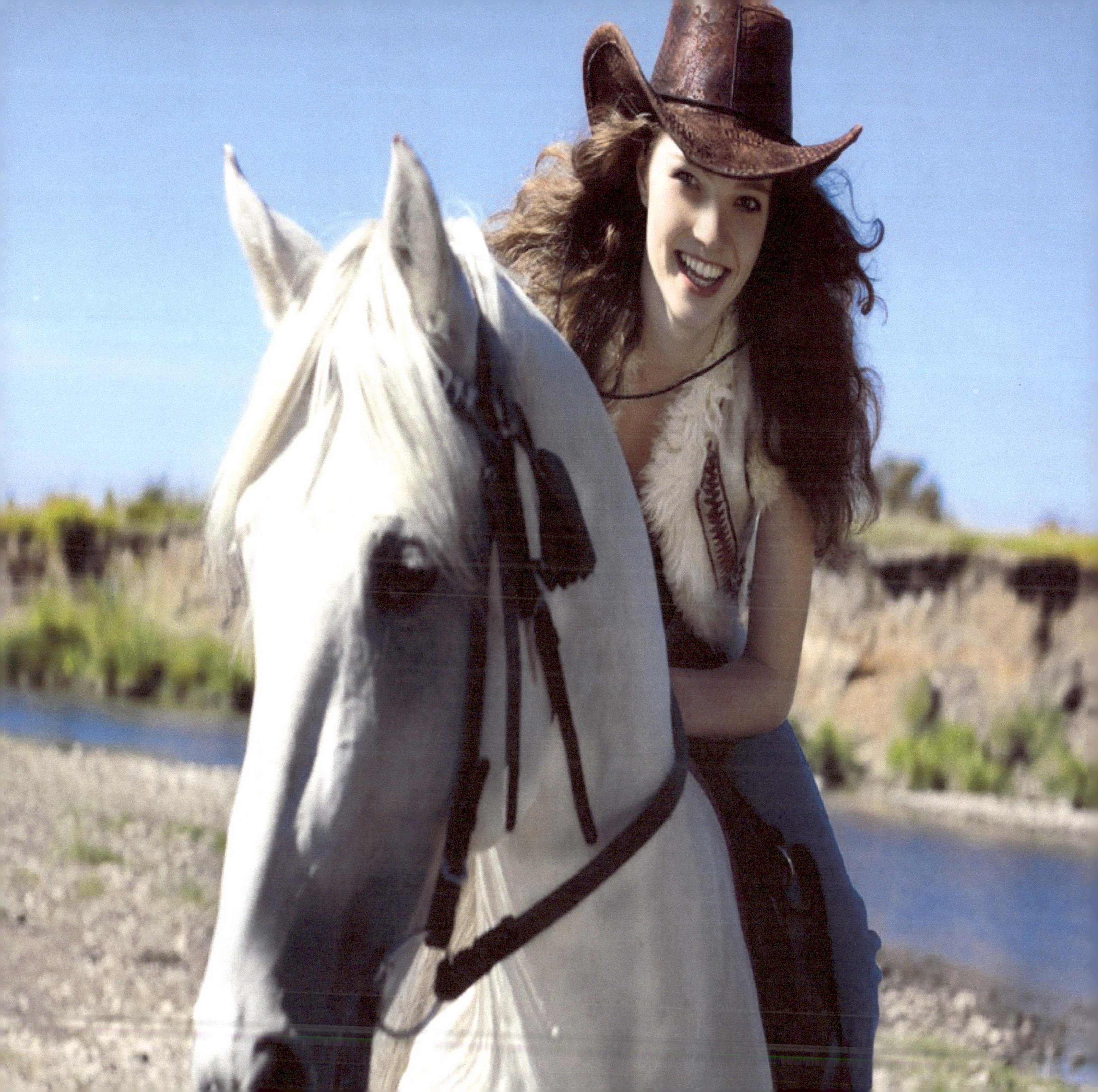

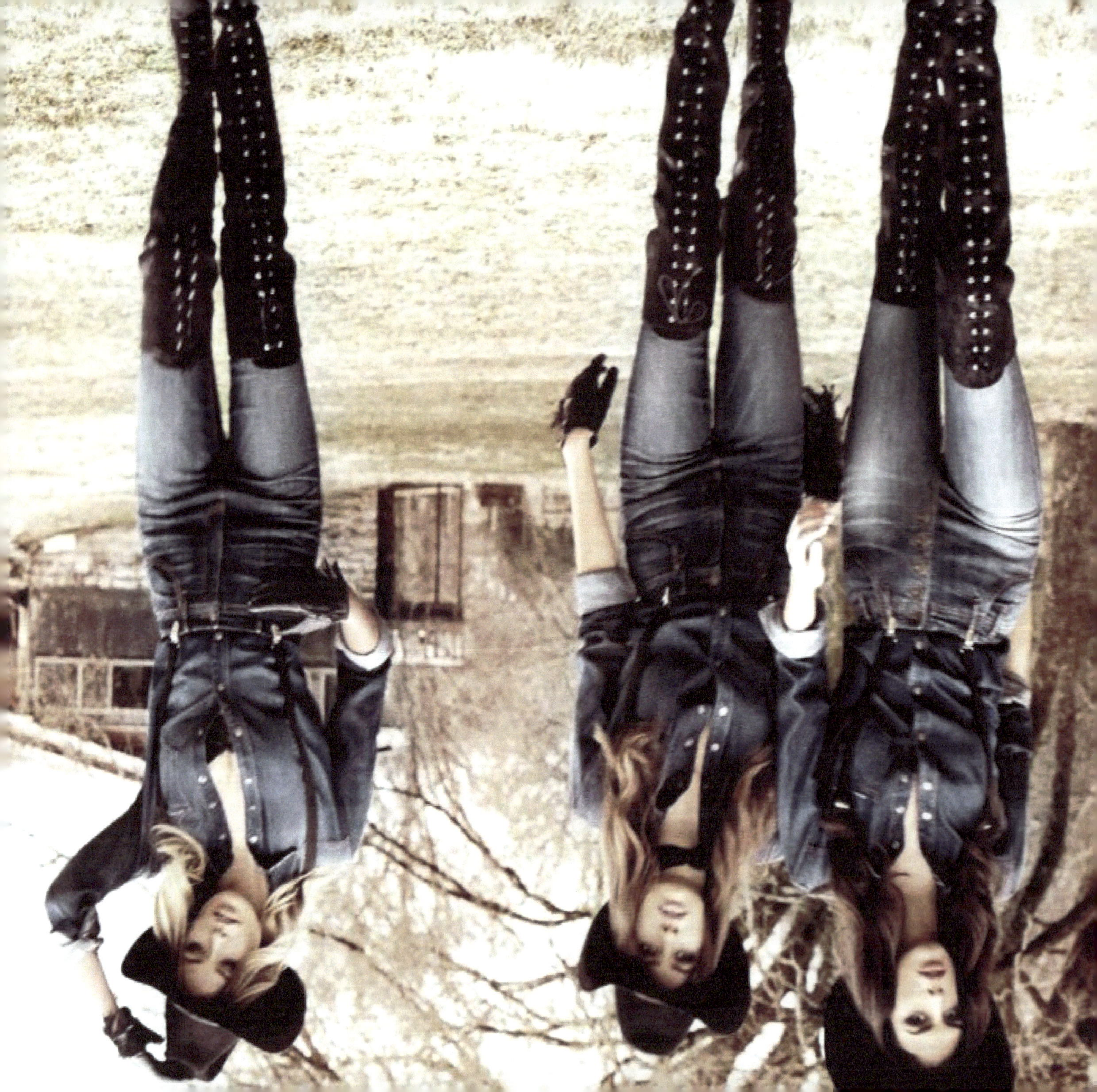